Book 1
Android Programming In a Day!

BY SAM KEY

&

Book 2
CSS Programming
Professional Made Easy

BY SAM KEY

Book 1
Android Programming In a Day!
BY SAM KEY

The Power Guide for Beginners In Android App Programming

Programming Box Set #82: Android Programming in a Day & CSS Programming Professional Made Easy

Table Of Contents

Introduction

I want to thank you and congratulate you for purchasing the book, "Introduction to Android Programming in a Day – The Power Guide for Beginners in Android App Programming".

This book contains proven steps and strategies on how to get started with Android app development.

This book will focus on preparing you with the fun and tiring world of Android app development. Take note that this book will not teach you on how to program. It will revolve around the familiarization of the Android SDK and Eclipse IDE.

Why not focus on programming immediately? Unfortunately, the biggest reason many aspiring Android developers stop on learning this craft is due to the lack of wisdom on the Android SDK and Eclipse IDE.

Sure, you can also make apps using other languages like Python and other IDEs on the market. However, you can expect that it is much more difficult than learning Android's SDK and Eclipse's IDE.

On the other hand, you can use tools online to develop your Android app for you. But where's the fun in that? You will not learn if you use such tools. Although it does not mean that you should completely stay away from that option.

Anyway, the book will be split into four chapters. The first will prepare you and tell you the things you need before you develop apps. The second will tell you how you can configure your project. The third will introduce you to the Eclipse IDE. And the last chapter will teach you on how to run your program in your Android device.

Also, this book will be sprinkled with tidbits about the basic concepts of Android app development. And as you read along, you will have an idea on what to do next.

Thanks again for purchasing this book, I hope you enjoy it!

Chapter 1: Preparation

Android application development is not easy. You must have some decent background in program development. It is a plus if you know Visual Basic and Java. And it will be definitely a great advantage if you are familiar or have already used Eclipse's IDE (Integrated Development Environment). Also, being familiar with XML will help you.

You will need a couple of things before you can start developing apps.

First, you will need a high-end computer. It is common that other programming development kits do not need a powerful computer in order to create applications. However, creating programs for Android is a bit different. You will need more computing power for you to run Android emulators, which are programs that can allow you to test your programs in your computer.

Using a weak computer without a decent processor and a good amount of RAM will only make it difficult for you to run those emulators. If you were able to run it, it will run slowly.

Second, you will need an Android device. That device will be your beta tester. With it, you will know how your program will behave in an Android device. When choosing the test device, make sure that it is at par with the devices of the market you are targeting for your app. If you are targeting tablet users, use a tablet. If you are targeting smartphones, then use a smartphone.

Third, you will need the Android SDK (Software Development Kit) from Google. The SDK is a set of files and programs that can allow you to create and compile your program's code. As of this writing, the latest Android SDK's file size is around 350mb. It will take you 15 – 30 minutes to download it. If you uncompressed the Android SDK file, it will take up around 450mb of your computer's disk space. The link to the download page is: http://developer.android.com/sdk/index.html

The SDK can run on Windows XP, Windows 7, Mac OSX 10.8.5 (or higher), and Linux distros that can run 32bit applications and has glibc (GNU C library) 2.11 or higher.

Once you have unpacked the contents of the file you downloaded, open the SDK Manager. That program is the development kit's update tool. To make sure you have the latest versions of the kit's components, run the manager once in a while and download those updates. Also, you can use the SDK Manager to download older versions of SDK. You must do that in case you want to make programs with devices with dated Android operating systems.

Chapter 2: Starting Your First Project

To start creating programs, you will need to open Eclipse. The Eclipse application file can be found under the eclipse folder on the extracted files from the Android SDK. Whenever you run Eclipse, it will ask you where you want your Eclipse workspace will be stored. You can just use the default location and just toggle the don't show checkbox.

New Project

To start a new Android application project, just click on the dropdown button of the New button on Eclipse's toolbar. A context menu will appear, and click on the Android application project.

The New Android Application project details window will appear. In there, you will need to input some information for your project. You must provide your program's application name, project name, and package name. Also, you can configure the minimum and target SDK where your program can run and the SDK that will be used to compile your code. And lastly, you can indicate the default theme that your program will use.

Application Name

The application name will be the name that will be displayed on the Google's Play Store when you post it there. The project name will be more of a file name for Eclipse. It will be the project's identifier. It should be unique for every project that you build in Eclipse. By default, Eclipse will generate a project and package name for your project when you type something in the Application Name text box.

Package Name

The package name is not usually displayed for users. Take note that in case you will develop a large program, you must remember that your package name should never be changed. On the other hand, it is common that package names are the reverse of your domain name plus your project's name. For example, if your website's domain name is www.mywebsite.com and your project's name is Hello World, a good package name for your project will be com.mywebsite.helloworld.

The package name should follow the Java package name convention. The naming convention is there to prevent users from having similar names, which could result to numerous conflicts. Some of the rules you need to follow for the package name are:

•   Your package name should be all in lower caps. Though Eclipse will accept a package name with a capital letter, but it is still best to adhere to standard practice.

•   The reverse domain naming convention is included as a standard practice.

•   Avoid using special characters in the package name. Instead, you can replace it with underscores.

•   Also, you should never use or include the default com.example in your package name. Google Play will not accept an app with a package name like that.

Minimum SDK

Minimum required SDK could be set to lower or the lowest version of Android. Anything between the latest and the set minimum required version can run your program. Setting it to the lowest, which is API 1 or Android 1.0, can make your target audience wider.

Setting it to Android 2.2 (Froyo) or API 8, can make your program run on almost 95% of all Android devices in the world. The drawback fn this is that the features you can include in your program will be limited. Adding new features will force your minimum required SDK to move higher since some of the new functions in Android is not available on lower versions of the API (Application Programming Interface).

Target SDK

The target SDK should be set to the version of Android that most of your target audience uses. It indicates that you have tested your program to that version. And it means that your program is fully functional if they use it on a device that runs the target Android version.

Whenever a new version of Android appears, you should also update the target SDK of your program. Of course, before you release it to the market again, make sure that you test it on an updated device.

If a device with the same version as your set target SDK runs your program, it will not do any compatibility behavior or adjust itself to run the program. By default, you should set it to the highest version to attract your potential app buyers. Setting a lower version for your target SDK would make your program old and dated. By the way, the target SDK should be always higher or equal with the minimum target SDK version.

Compile with

The compile with version should be set to the latest version of Android. This is to make sure that your program will run on almost all versions down to the minimum version you have indicated, and to take advantage of the newest features and optimization offered by the latest version of Android. By default, the Android SDK will only have one version available for this option, which is API 20 or Android 4.4 (KitKat Wear).

After setting those all up, it is time to click on the Next button. The new page in the screen will contain some options such as creating custom launcher icon and creating activity. As of now, you do not need to worry about those. Just leave the default values and check, and click the Next button once again.

Custom Launcher Icon

Since you have left the Create Custom Launcher option checked, the next page will bring you in the launcher icon customization page. In there, you will be given three options on how you would create your launcher. Those options are launcher icons made from an image, clipart, or text.

With the text and clipart method, you can easily create an icon you want without thinking about the size and quality of the launcher icon. With those two, you can just get a preset image from the SDK or Android to use as a launcher icon. The same goes with the text method since all you need is to type the letters you want to appear on the icon and the SDK will generate an icon based on that.

The launcher icon editor also allows you to change the background and foreground color of your icon. Also, you can scale the text and clipart by changing the value of the additional padding of the icon. And finally, you can add simple 3D shapes on your icon to make it appear more professional.

Bitmap Iconography Tips

When it comes to images, you need to take note of a few reminders. First, always make sure that you will use vector images. Unlike the typical bitmap images (pictures taken from cameras or images created using Paint), vector images provide accurate and sharp images. You can scale it multiple times, but its sharpness will not disappear and will not pixelate. After all, vector images do not contain information about pixels. It only has numbers and location of the colors and lines that will appear in it. When it is scaled, it does not perform antialiasing or stretching since its image will be mathematically rendered.

In case that you will be the one creating or designing the image that you will use for your program and you will be creating a bitmap image, make sure that you start with a large image. A large image is easier to create and design.

Also, since in Android, multiple sizes of your icon will be needed, a large icon can make it easier for you to make smaller ones. Take note that if you scale a big picture into a small one, some details will be lost, but it will be easier to edit and fix and it will still look crisp. On the other hand, if you scale a small image into a big one, it will pixelate and insert details that you do not intend to show such as jagged and blurred edges.

Nevertheless, even when scaling down a big image into a smaller one, do not forget to rework the image. Remember that a poor-looking icon makes people think that the app you are selling is low-quality. And again, if you do not want to go through all that, create a vector image instead.

Also, when you create an image, make sure that it will be visible in any background. Aside from that, it is advisable to make it appear uniform with other Android icons. To do that, make sure that your image has a distinct silhouette that will make it look like a 3D image. The icon should appear as if you were looking above it and as if the source of light is on top of the image. The topmost part of the icon should appear lighter and the bottom part should appear darker.

Activity

Once you are done with your icon, click on the Next button. The page will now show the Activity window. It will provide you with activity templates to work on. The window has a preview box where you can see what your app will look like for every activity template. Below the selection, there is a description box that will tell you what each template does. For now, select the Blank Activity and click Next. The next page will ask you some details regarding the activity. Leave it on its default values and click Finish.

Once you do that, Eclipse will setup your new project. It might take a lot of time, especially if you are using a dated computer. The next chapter will discuss the programming interface of Eclipse.

Chapter 3: Getting Familiar with Eclipse and Contents of an Android App

When Eclipse has finished its preparation, you will be able to start doing something to your program. But hold onto your horses; explore Eclipse first before you start fiddling with anything.

Editing Area

In the middle of the screen, you will see a preview of your program. In it, you will see your program's icon beside the title of your program. Just left of it is the palette window. It contains all the elements that you can place in your program.

Both of these windows are inside Eclipse's editing area. You will be spending most of your time here, especially if you are going to edit or view something in your code or layout.

The form widgets tab will be expanded in the palette by default. There you will see the regular things you see in an Android app such as buttons, radio buttons, progress bar (the circle icon that spins when something is loading in your device or the bar the fills up when your device is loading), seek bar, and the ratings bar (the stars you see in reviews).

Aside from the form widgets, there are other elements that you can check and use. Press the horizontal tabs or buttons and examine all the elements you can possibly use in your program.

To insert a widget in your program, you can just drag the element you want to include from the palette and drop it in your program's preview. Eclipse will provide you visual markers and grid snaps for you to place the widgets you want on the exact place you want. Easy, right?

Take note, some of the widgets on the palette may require higher-level APIs or versions of Android. For example, the Grid Layout from the Layouts section of the palette requires API 14 (Android 4.0 Ice Cream Sandwich) or higher. If you add it in your program, it will ask you if you want to install it. In case you did include and install it, remember that it will not be compatible for older versions or any device running on API 13 and lower. It is advisable that you do not include any element that asks for installation. It might result into errors.

Output Area, Status Bar, and Problem Browser

On the bottom part of Eclipse, the status bar, problem browser, and output area can be found. It will contain messages regarding to the state of your project. If Eclipse found errors in your program, it will be listed there. Always check the Problems bar for any issues. Take note that you cannot run or compile your program if Eclipse finds at least one error on your project.

Navigation Pane

On the leftmost part of your screen is the navigation pane that contains the package explorer. The package explorer lets you browse all the files that are included in your project. Three of the most important files that you should know where to look for are:

•   activity_main.xml: This file is your program's main page or window. And it will be the initial file that will be opened when you create a new project. In case you accidentally close it on your editor window, you can find it at: YourProjectName > res > layout > activity_main.xml.

• MainActivity.java: As of now, you will not need to touch this file. However, it is important to know where it is since later in your Android development activities, you will need to understand it and its contents. It is located at: YourProjectName > src > YourPackageName > MainActivity.java.

• AndroidManifest.xml: It contains the essential information that you have set up a while ago when you were creating your project file in Eclipse. You can edit the minimum and target SDK in there. It is located at YourProjectName > AndroidManifest.xml.

Aside from those files, you should take note of the following directories:

• src/: This is where most of your program's source files will be placed. And your main activity file is locafile is located.

• res/: Most of the resources will be placed here. The resources are placed inside the subdirectories under this folder.

• res/drawable-hdpi/: Your high density bitmap files that you might show in your app will go in here.

• res/layout/: All the pages or interface in your app will be located here – including your activity_main.xml.

• res/values/: The values you will store and use in your program will be placed in this directory in form of XML files.

In the event that you will create multiple projects, remember that the directory for those other projects aside from the one you have opened will still be available in your package explorer. Because of that, you might get confused over the files you are working on. Thankfully, Eclipse's title bar indicates the location and name of the file you are editing, which makes it easier to know what is currently active on the editing area.

Outline Box

Displays the current structure of the file you are editing. The outline panel will help you visualize the flow and design of your app. Also, it can help you find the widgets you want to edit.

Properties Box

Whenever you are editing a layout file, the properties box will appear below the outline box. With the properties box, you can edit certain characteristics of a widget. For example, if you click on the Hello World text on the preview of your main activity layout file, the contents of the properties box will be populated. In there, you can edit the properties of the text element that you have clicked. You can change the text, height, width, and even its font color.

Menu and Toolbar

The menu bar contains all the major functionalities of Eclipse. In case you do not know where the button of a certain tool is located, you can just invoke that tool's function on the menu bar. On the other hand, the tool bar houses all the major functions in Eclipse. The most notable buttons there are the New, Save, and Run.

As of now, look around Eclipse's interface. Also, do not do or change anything on the main activity file or any other file. The next chapter will discuss about how to run your program. As of now, the initial contents of your project are also valid as an android program. Do not change anything since you might produce an unexpected error. Nevertheless, if you really do want to change something, go ahead. You can just create another project for you to keep up with the next chapter.

Chapter 4: Running Your Program

By this time, even if you have not done anything yet to your program, you can already run and test it in your Android device or emulator. Why teach this first before the actual programming? Well, unlike typical computer program development, Android app development is a bit bothersome when it comes to testing.

First, the program that you are developing is intended for Android devices. You cannot actually run it normally in your computer without the help of an emulator. And you will actually do a lot of testing. Even with the first lines of code or changes in your program, you will surely want to test it.

Second, the Android emulator works slow. Even with good computers, the emulator that comes with the Android SDK is painstakingly sluggish. Alternatively, you can use BlueStacks. BlueStacks is a free Android emulator that works better than the SDK's emulator. It can even run games with it! However, it is buggy and does not work well (and does not even run sometimes) with every computer.

This chapter will focus on running your program into your Android device. You will need to have a USB data cable and connect your computer and Android. Also, you will need to have the right drivers for your device to work as a testing platform for the programs you will develop. Unfortunately, this is the preferred method for most beginners since running your app on Android emulators can bring a lot more trouble since it is super slow. And that might even discourage you to continue Android app development.

Why Android Emulators are Slow

**Programming Box Set #82: Android Programming in a Day & CSS
Programming Professional Made Easy**

Why are Android emulators slow? Computers can run virtual OSs
without any problems, but why cannot the Android emulator work
fine? Running virtual OSs is not something as resource-extensive
anymore with today's computer standards. However, with Android,
you will actually emulate an OS together with a mobile device. And
nowadays, these mobile devices are as powerful as some of the dated
computers back then. Regular computers will definitely have a hard
time with that kind of payload from an Android emulator.

USB Debugging Mode

To run your program in an Android device, connect your Android to
your computer. After that, set your Android into USB debugging
mode. Depending on the version of the Android device you are using,
the steps might change.

For 3.2 and older Android devices:

Go to Settings > Applications > Development

For 4.0 and newer Android devices:

Go to Settings > Developer Options

For 4.2 and newer Android devices with hidden Developer Options:

Go to Settings > About Phone. After that, tap the Build Number seven
times. Go back to the previous screen. The Developer Options should
be visible now.

Android Device Drivers

When USB debugging is enabled, your computer will install the right
drivers for the Android device that you have. If your computer does
not have the right drivers, you will not be able to run your program on

your device. If that happens to you, visit this page: http://developer.android.com/tools/extras/oem-usb.html. It contains instructions on how you can install the right driver for your device and operating system.

Running an App in Your Android Device Using Eclipse

Once your device is already connected and you have the right drivers for it, you can now do a test run of your application. On your Eclipse window, click the Run button on the toolbar or in the menu bar.

If a Run As window appeared, select the Android Application option and click on the OK button. After that, a dialog box will appear. It will provide you with two options: running the program on an Android device or on an AVD (Android Virtual Device) or emulator.

If your device was properly identified by your computer, it will appear on the list. Click on your device's name and click OK. Eclipse will compile your Android app, install it on your device, and then run it. That is how simple it is.

Take note, there will be times that your device will appear offline on the list. In case that happens, there are two simple fixes that you can do to make it appear online again: restart your device or disable and enable the USB debugging function on your device.

Now, you can start placing widgets on your main activity file. However, always make sure that you do not place any widgets that require higher APIs.

Conclusion

Thank you again for purchasing this book!

I hope this book was able to help you get started with Android Programming in a Day!.

The next step is to study the following:

View and Viewgroups: View and Viewgroups are the two types of objects that you will be dealing with Android. View objects are the elements or widgets that you see in Android programs. Viewgroup objects act as containers to those View objects.

Relative, Linear, and Table Layout: When it comes to designing your app, you need to know the different types of layouts. In later versions of Android, you can use other versions of layouts, but of course, the API requirements will go up if you use them. Master these, and you will be able to design faster and cleaner.

Adding Activities or Interface: Of course, you would not want your program to contain one page only. You need more. You must let your app customers to see more content and functions. In order to do that, you will need to learn adding activities to your program. This is the part when developing your Android app will be tricky. You will not be able to rely completely on the drag and drop function and graphical layout view of Eclipse. You will need to start typing some code into your program.

Adding the Action Bar: The action bar is one of the most useful elements in Android apps. It provides the best location for the most used functions in your program. And it also aid your users when switching views, tabs, or drop down list.

Once you have gain knowledge on those things, you will be able to launch a decent app on the market. The last thing you might want to do is to learn how to make your program support other Android devices.

You must know very well that Android devices come in all shapes and form. An Android device can be a tablet, a smartphone, or even a television. Also, they come with different screen sizes. You cannot just expect that all your customers will be using a 4-inch display smartphone. Also, you should think about the versions of Android they are using. Lastly, you must also add language options to your programs. Even though English is fine, some users will appreciate if your program caters to the primary language that they use.

And that is about it for this book. Make sure you do not stop learning Android app development.

Finally, if you enjoyed this book, please take the time to share your thoughts and post a review on Amazon. We do our best to reach out to readers and provide the best value we can. Your positive review will help us achieve that. It'd be greatly appreciated!

Thank you and good luck!

Book 2
CSS Programming
Professional Made Easy
BY SAM KEY

Expert CSS Programming Language Success in a Day for any Computer User!

Table of Contents

Introduction

I want to thank you and congratulate you for purchasing the book, "Professional CSS Programming Made Easy: Expert CSS Programming Language Success In A Day for any Computer User!".

This book contains proven steps and strategies on how to effectively apply CSS style rules in making your webpages more appealing to your readers. In this book, the different aspects of CSS programming are discussed in simple language to make it easy for you to understand even if you have no previous experience in programming. In no time, you can start creating your own CSS style rules!

Thanks again for purchasing this book, I hope you enjoy it!

Chapter 1: What is CSS?

CSS is short for Cascading Style Sheets which is a simple design language that is meant to streamline the enhancement of web page presentations. Basically, through CSS, you will be able to manage how a web page looks and feels. When you use CSS, you will be able to control the background color or image in the web page, the color of the texts, the style of the font, the size of the columns, the column layout, the spacing in between paragraphs and a whole lot more of design effects.

Even though CSS is quite simple to understand, it can provide you with great control of how an HTML document is presented. People who study CSS often study other markup languages such as XHTML or HTML.

What are the advantages of CSS?

- CSS will allow you to save time. After you have written a CSS code once, you can then use the same sheet in various web pages. You can create a style for each web page element and then use it to as many HTML pages as you desire in the future.

- Your web pages will load faster. If you will use CSS in your web pages, you no longer have to write an HTML tag attribute all the time. You simple create 1 CSS rule of a tag and then use it for all the incidences of that specific tag. When you use less HTML codes, it translates to faster download speed.

- Your web pages become easier to maintain. If you wish to create a global change in your website, all you need to do is adjust the style and then all the elements included in your different web pages will be automatically adjusted.

- You will be able to enjoy better styles compared to HTML. The style attributes available for HTML codes are lesser compared to what you can work with when you use CSS. This means that you will be able to create top quality styles for your web pages.

- You will have multiple device compatibility. With CSS, you will be allowed to use content that can be optimized for different types of device. Even when you use the same HTML document, you can present the website in various versions for different devices such as mobile phones, tablets, desktop and even printing.

- You will be able to adopt web standards that are recognized globally. More and more people are losing interest in using HTML attributes and have started to recommend the use of CSS.

- You get to future-proof. By using CSS in your web pages now, you can also ensure that they will have compatibility with future browsers.

Creation and Maintenance of CSS

Only a small group of people within the World Wide Web Consortium (W3C) referred to as the CSS Working Group is allowed to create and maintain CSS. This group generates the CSS specifications which are then submitted to the W3C members for discussion and ratification. Only ratified specifications are given the recommendation signal by the W3C. You need to note that they are referred to as recommendations since the W3C cannot really dictate how the language is to be actually implementation. The software the implement the CSS language is created by independent organizations and companies.

Note: If you wish to know, yes, the W3C is the group that provides the recommendations on how the Internet should work and how it should progress.

Different CSS Versions

The W3C released CSS1 or Cascading Style Sheets Level 1was released as a recommendation in 1996. The recommendation included a description of the CSS together with a basic visual formatting model that can be used for every HTML tag.

Programming Box Set #82: Android Programming in a Day & CSS Programming Professional Made Easy

In May 1998, the W3C released the recommendation for CSS2 or Cascading Style Sheets Level 2 which included further information that builds on CSS1. CSS2 added support for style sheets for specific media such as aural devices, printers, element tables and positioning and downloadable fonts.

Chapter 2: Various Types of CSS Selectors

A CSS is composed of different style rules that are translated by the browser for them to be applied to the specific elements in your web page. A style rule is further composed of 3 parts: selector, property and value. A selector is the HTML tag wherein the style rule will be applied. Examples include <table> or <h1>. A property is the specific attribute type that an HTML tag has. In simple terms, you could say that each HTML attribute is ultimately translated to a CSS property. Examples of properties include border or color. Values, on the other hand, are directly assigned to the properties. For instance, for the color property, you can assign a value of #000000 or black.

One way to write a CSS Style Rule Syntax is: Selector (property: value)

Ex. You can write the syntax rule for a table border as: table (border: 2px solid #C00;). The selector in this example is table while the property is the border. The specific value given for the property is 2px solid #C00.

In this chapter, we will be talking about the different kinds of selectors.

Type Selector

The selector in the example given above (table) is categorized under the Type Selector. Another example of a type Selector is "level 1 heading" or "h1"). We can write a CSS Style Rule Syntax as: h1 (color: #36CFFF;). The selector in this example is h1 while the property is the color. The specific value given for the property is #36CFFF.

Universal Selector

This is designated by an asterisk (*) which means that the style rule syntax that you want to create will be applied to all elements in your webpage and not only to specific elements.

Example: *(color: #FFFFFF;). This style rule means that you want all of the elements (including fonts, borders, etc.) in your webpage to be white.

Descendant Selector

You use the descendant selector when you wish to apply a certain style rule for a specific element that lies within a specific element.

Example: ul em (color:#FFFFFF;), the value #FFFFFF (white) will only be applied to the property (color) if the selector/property <em> lies within the selector <ul>.

Class Selector

Using the Class Selector, you will be able to define a specific style rule that can be applied based on the specific class attribute of elements. This means that all of the elements that have that specific class attributed will have the same formatting as specified in the style rule.

Example 1: .white (color: #FFFFFF;). Here the class attribute is "white" and it means that the color "white" will be applied to all of the elements given the class attribute "white" in your document.

Example 2: h1.white (color: #FFFFFF;). This style rule is more specific. The class attribute is still "white" and the style rule will be applied to the elements given the class attribute "white" but ONLY if they are ALSO an <h1> or "level 1 heading" element.

You can actually give one or more class selectors for each element. For example, you can give the class selectors "center" and "bold" to a paragraph <p> by writing it as <p class="center,bold">.

ID Selector

You use an ID selector to create a style rule that is based on the specific ID attribute of the element. This means that all of the elements that have that specific ID will have the same format as defined in the style rule.

Example 1: #white (color: #FFFFFF;). The ID assigned here is "white" and the style rule means that all elements with the "white" ID attribute will be rendered black in your document.

Example 2: h1#white (color: #FFFFFF;). This is more specific because it means that the style rule will only be applied to elements with the ID attribute "white" ONLY IF they are a level 1 heading element.

The ID selectors are ideally used as foundations for descendant selectors. Example: #white h3 (color: #FFFFFF;). The style rule dictates that all level 3 headings located in the different pages of your website will be displayed in white color ONLY IF those level 3 headings are within tags that have an ID attribute of "white".

Child Selector

The Child Selector is quite similar to the Descendant Selector except that they have different functionalities.

Example: body > p (color: #FFFFFF;). The style rule states that a paragraph will be rendered in white if it is a direct child of the <body> element. If the paragraph is within other elements such as <td> or <div>, the style rule will not apply to it.

Attribute Selector

You can apply specific styles to your webpage elements that have specific attributes.

Example: input(type="text"](color: #FFFFFF;).

One benefit of the above example is that the specified color in the style rule will only affect your desired text field and will not affect the <input type="submit"/>.

You need to keep the following rules in mind when using attribute selectors:

• p[lang]. All elements of the paragraph that has a "lang" attribute will be selected.

- p[lang="fr"]. All elements of the paragraph that has a "lang" attribute AND the value "fr" in the "lang" attribute will be selected. Note that the value should exactly be "fr".

- p[lang~="fr"]. All elements of the paragraph that has a "lang" attribute AND CONTAINS the value "fr" in the "lang" attribute will be selected.

- p[lang |="ne"]. All elements of the paragraph that has a "lang" attribute AND CONTAINS value that is EITHER exactly "en" or starts with "en-" in the "lang" attribute will be selected.

Multiple Style Rules

It is possible for you to create multiple style rules for one specific element. The style rules can be defined in such a way that different properties are combined into a single block and specific values are assigned to each property.

Example 1:

h1(color: #35C; font-weight: bold; letter-spacing: .5em; margin-bottom: 1em; text-transform: uppercase;)

You will note that the properties and their corresponding values are separated from other property/value pairs by using a semi-colon. You can opt to write the combine style rules as a single line similar to the example above or as multiple lines for better readability. The example below is just the same as Example 1:

Example 2:

h1 (

color: #35C;

font-weight: bold;

letter-spacing: .5em;

margin-bottom: 1em;

text-transform: uppercase;

)

How to Group Selectors

You can actually apply one single style to different selectors. All you really need to do is write all the selectors at the start of your style rule but make sure that they are separated by a comma. The examples above both pertain to the selector or property "level 1 heading". If you want to apply the same style rule to "level 2 heading" and "level 3 heading", you can include h2 and h3 in the first line, as follows:

Example:

h1, h2, h3 (

color: #35C;

font-weight: bold;

letter-spacing: .5em;

margin-bottom: 1em;

text-transform: uppercase;

)

Note that the sequence of the selector element is not relevant. You can write it as h3,h2,h1 and the style rule will exactly be the same. It means that the specified style rules will still be applied to all the elements of the selectors.

It is also possible to create a style rule that combines different class selectors.

Example:

#supplement, #footer, #content (

position: absolute;

left: 520px;

width: 210px;

**Programming Box Set #82: Android Programming in a Day & CSS
Programming Professional Made Easy**

)

Chapter 3: Methods of Associating Styles

There are actually 4 methods of associating styles within an HTML document – Embedded CSS, Inline CSS, External CSS and Imported CSS. But the two most frequently used are Inline CSS and External CSS.

Embedded CSS

This method uses the <style> element wherein the tags are positioned within the <head>...</head> tags. All elements that exist within your document will be affected by a rule that has been written using this syntax. The generic syntax is as follows:

<head>

<style type="text/css" media="...">

Style Rules

. . . .

</style>

</head>

The following attributes that are connected to the <style> element are as follows:

•   Type with value "text/css". This attribute indicates the style sheet language as a content-type (MIME type). You need to note that this attribute is always required.

•   Media with values as "screen", "tty", "tv", "projection", "handheld", "print", "braille", "aural" or "all". This attribute indicates what kind of device the webpage will be shown. This attribute is only optional and it always has "all" as a default value.

 Example:

```
<head>

<style type="text/css" media="screen">

h2(

color: #38C;

)

</style>

</head>
```

Inline CSS

This method uses the style attribute of a specific HTML element in defining the style rule. This means that the style rule will only be applied to the specific HTML element ONLY. The generic syntax is as follows: <element style=". . .style rules. . . .">

Only one attribute is connected to the <style> attribute and it is as follows:

•   Style with value "style rules". The value that you will specify for the style attribute is basically a combination of various style declarations. You should use a semicolon to separate the different style declarations.

Example:

<h2 style ="color:#000;">. This is inline CSS </h2>

External CSS

This method uses the <link> element in defining the style rule. You can use it to add external style sheets within your webpage. The external style sheet that you will add will have a different text file that has the extension .css. All the style rules that you want to apply to your webpage elements will be added inside the external text file and then you can append the text file in any of your web pages by creating the <link> element. The general syntax that you will be using will be:

```
<head>
```

```
<link type="text/css" href=" . . ." media=" . . ." />
```

```
</head>
```

The following attributes that are connected with the <style> elements are as follows:

• Type with the value "text/css". This indicates that you are using a MIME type or a content type for your style sheet language. Note that you are always required to use this attribute.

• Href with value "URL". This attribute will indicate the specific style sheet file that contains your style rules. Again, you are also always required to use this attribute.

• Media with value "screen", "tty", "tv", "projection", "handheld", "print", "braille", "aural" or "all". This attribute indicates the specific media device that you will use to display the document. This attribute is only optional and it has a default value of "all".

Example wherein the style sheet file is named as docstyle.css:

```
h2, h3 (
```

```
color: #38C;
```

```
font-weight: bold;
```

```
letter-spacing: .5em;
```

```
margin-bottom: 2em;
```

```
text-transform: uppercase;
```

```
)
```

Then you can add your style sheet file "docstyle.css" in your webpage by adding these rules:

```
<head>
```

```
<link type="text/css" href="docstyle.css" media="all" />
```

```
</head>
```

Imported CSS

This method which uses the @import rule is the same as the <link> element because it is used to import an external style sheet file to your webpage. The generic syntax of this method is as follows:

<head>

<@import "URL";

</head>

Here is another alternative syntax that you can use:

<head>

<@import url ("URL");

</head>

Example:

<head>

@import "docstyle.css'"

</head>

How to Override CSS Style Rules

The following can override the style rules that you have created using the above four methods:

•   An inline style sheet is given the number one priority. This means that an inline style sheet will always supersede a rule that has been written with a <style>...</style> tag or a rule that has been defined in an external stylesheet file.

•   A rule that has been written with a <style>...</style> tag will always supersede a style rule that has been defined in an external stylesheet file.

•   The rules that you define within an external stylesheet file is always given the lowest priority. This means that any rules defined within the external file will only be applied if the 2 rules above aren't valid.

How to Handle an Old Browser:

Currently, there are a lot of old browsers that are not yet capable of supporting CSS. When you are working with these kind of browsers, you need to write your embedded CSS within the HTML document. Here is an example on how you can embed CSS in an old browser:

<style type="text/css">

<!—

Body, td (

   Color: red;

)

-->

</style>

How to Add a CSS Comment

In case it is necessary for you to include an additional comment within the style sheet block, you can easily do this by writing your comment within /*....this is a comment in style sheet....*/. The /*....*/ method used in C++ and C programming languages can also be used in adding comments in a multi-line block.

Example:

/* This is an external style sheet file */

Programming Box Set #82: Android Programming in a Day & CSS Programming Professional Made Easy

```
h3, h2, h1 (

color: #38C;

font-weight: bold;

letter-spacing: .5em;

margin-bottom: 2em;

text-transform: uppercase;

)
/* end of style rules. */
```

Chapter 4: Measurement Units

There are several measurements that CSS can support. These include absolute units like inch, centimeter, points, etc. They also include relative measures like em unit and percentage. These values are important when you want to specify the different measurements you want to include in your style rule. Example:

border="2px solid black".

Here are the most common measurements that you will use in creating CSS style rules:

Unit of Measure	Description	Example
%	Indicates measurements as a percentage in relation to another value which is normally an enclosing element	p {font-size: 12pt; line-height: 150%;}
cm	Indicates measurements in centimeter	div {margin-bottom: 1.5cm;}
em	A relative number used in measuring font height using em spaces. One em unit is equal to the size of a particular font. This means, if you want a certain font to have a size of 10pt, one "em" unit is equal to 10pt and 3em is equal to 30pt.	p {letter-spacing: 6em;}
ex	A number used to define a measurement in relation to the x-height of a font. The x-height is defined by the height of letter x in lowercase in any	p {font-size: 20pt: line-height: 2ex;}

	given font.	
in	Indicates measurements in inches	p {word-spacing: .12in;}
mm	Indicates measurements in millimeter	p {word-spacing: 12mm;}
pc	Indicates measurements in picas. One pica is equal to 12 points. This means that there are six picas in one inch.	p {font-size: 18pc;}
pt	Indicates measurements in points. One point is equal to 1/72 of one inch.	body {font-size: 20pt;}
px	Indicates measurements in screen pixel	p {padding: 32px;}

Chapter 5: Style Rules Using Colors

A color in CSS style rules is indicated by color values. Normally, the color values are used to define the color of either the background of an element or its foreground (that is, its text). You can also utilize colors to change how your borders and other aesthetic effects look.

Color values in CSS rules can be specified using the following formats:

•   Hex code using the syntax #RRGGBB. Example: p {color: #FFFF00;}. The six digits represent one specific color wherein RR represents the value for red, GG the value for green and BB the value for blue. You can get the hexadecimal values of different colors from graphics software such as Jasc Paintshop Pro and Adobe Photoshop. You can also use the Advanced Paint Brush to get the hexadecimal values. You need to note that the six digits should always be preceded by the hash or pound sign (#).

•   Short hex code using the syntax #RGB. Example: p {color: #7A6;}. This is the shorter version of the hexadecimal value. You can also get them from Jasc Paintshop Pro, Adobe Photoshop or Advanced Paint Brush.

•   RGB % using the syntax rgb (rrr%, ggg%, bbb%). Example: p{color: rgb (40%, 50%, 40%);}. This format is actually advisable to use because not all browsers support this type of format.

•   RGB Absolute using the syntax rgb (rrr,ggg, bbb). Example: p {color: rgb (255,0,0);}

•   Keyword using the syntax black, aqua, etc. Example: p {color: red;}

Chapter 6: How to Set Backgrounds

What you will learn in this chapter includes how to define the background of the different elements in your web page. You can use any of the following background properties for specific elements in your webpage:

•   You can use the background color property to define the background color of your element.

•   You can use the background image property to define the background image of your element.

•   You can use the background repeat property to control whether your background image will be repeated or not.

•   You can use the background position property to control the position of the background image.

•   You can use the background attachment property to define whether your image is fixed or will scroll with the rest of the webpage.

•   You can use the background property to combine the above properties into one style rule.

Background Color

Here is a sample of how you can define the background color:

RED

This will result in RED.

Background Image

45

Here is a sample of how you can define the background image:

```
<table style="background-image:url (/images/pattern1.jpg);">
```

```
<tr><td>
```

The table now has an image in the background.

```
</td></tr>
```

```
</table>
```


How to Repeat a Background Image

In case your image is small, you can opt to repeat your background image. Otherwise, you can simple utilize the "no-repeat" value in the background-repeat property if you do not wish to have your background image repeated. This means that your image will only be displayed once. Note that "repeat value" is the default value in the background-repeat property.

Example:

```
<table style="background-image:url (/images/pattern2.jpg);

        background-repeat: repeat;">
```

```
<tr><td>
```

The background image in this table will be repeated several times.

```
</td></tr>
```

```
</table>
```


Here is a sample rule if you want the background image to be repeated vertically:

```
<table style="background-image:url (/images/pattern2.jpg);

        background-repeat: repeat-y;">
```

```
<tr><td>
```

The background image in this table will be repeated vertically.

</td></tr>

</table>

Here is a sample rule if you want the background image to be repeated horizontally:

<table style="background-image:url (/images/pattern2.jpg);

        background-repeat: repeat-x;">

<tr><td>

The background image in this table will be repeated horizontally.

</td></tr>

</table>

How to Set the Position of the Background Image

Here is a sample of how you can define the position of a background image at 150 pixels from the left side:

<table style="background-image: url (/images/pattern2.jpg);

        Background-position:150px;">

<tr><td>

The position of the background is now 150 pixels from the left side.

</td></tr>

</table>

Here is a sample of how you can define the position of a background image at 300 pixels from the top and 150 pixels from the left side:

Background-position:150px 300px;">

<tr><td>

The position of the background is now 300 pixels from the top and 150 pixels from the left side.

</td></tr>

</table>

How to Define the Background Attachment

The background attachment indicates whether the background image that you have set is fixed in its place or scrolls when you move the webpage.

Here is an example on how to write a style rule with a background image that is fixed:

<p style="background-image:url (/images/pattern2.jpg);

Background-attachment:fixed;">

The paragraph now has a background image that is fixed.

</p>

Here is an example on how to write a style rule with a background image that scrolls with the webpage:

<p style="background-image:url (/images/pattern2.jpg);

Background-attachment:scroll;">

The paragraph now has a background image that scrolls with the webpage.

</p>

How to Use the Shorthand Property

You can actually utilize the background property in order to define all of the background properties all at the same time.

Example:

The background image of this paragraph has a scroll and repeated properties.

Chapter 7: How to Set Font Properties

What you will learn in this chapter includes how to define the following font properties to a specific element in your webpage:

•   You can use the font family property to adjust the face of your selected font.

•   You can use the font style property to make your fonts either oblique or italic.

•   You can use the font variant property to include the "small caps" effect in your fonts.

•   You can use the font weight property to decrease or increase how light or bold your fonts are displayed.

•   You can use the font size property to decrease or increase the sizes of your fonts.

•   You can use the font property to define a combination of the font properties above.

How to Define the Font Family

Here is an example on how you can define the font family of a specific element. As value of the property, you can use any of the font family names available:

This message is displayed either in calibri, arial or the default serif font. It will depend on the existing fonts in your system.

How to Define the Font Style

Here is an example on how you can define the font style of a specific element. The values that you can use are oblique, italic or normal.

\

This message is displayed in oblique style.

\

How to Define the Font Variant

Here is an example on how you define the font variant of a specific element. The values that you can use are small-caps or normal.

\

This message is displayed in normal font variant.

\

How to Define the Font Weight

Here is an example on how you can define the font weight of a specific element. With this property, you will be able to define how bold you want your fonts to be. The values that you can use are bold, normal, lighter, bolder, 100, 200, 300, 400, 500, 600, 700, 800, and 900.

\

The font is displayed with normal font weight.

\

\

The font is displayed with lighter font weight.

\

\

The font is displayed with 800 font weight.

\

How to Define the Font Size

Here is an example on how you can define the font size of a specific element. With this property, you will be able to control the font sizes in your webpage. The values that you can use include small, medium, large, x-small, xx-small, xx-large, x-large, larger, smaller, size in % or size in pixels.

The font is displayed with 18 pixels font size.

The font is displayed with large font size.

The font is displayed with larger font size.

How to Define the Font Size Adjust

Here is an example on how you can define the font size adjust of a specific element. With this property, you will be able to adjust the x-height in order to make the legibility of your fonts better. The values that you can use include any number.

The font is displayed with 0.75 font size adjust value.

How to Define the Font Stretch

Here is an example on how you can define the font stretch of a specific element. With this property, you can allow the computer of your webpage readers to have a condensed or expanded version of the font you have defined in your elements. The values that you can use include normal, narrower, wider, condensed, extra-condensed, semi-condensed, ultra-condensed, semi-expanded, ultra-expanded, expanded and extra-expanded

If this does not seem to work, it is probably that the computer you are using does not have an expanded or condensed version of the font that was used.

How to Use the Shorthand Property

You can utilize the font property to define the font properties all at the same time.

Example:

This applies all of the defined properties on the text all at the same time.

Conclusion

Thank you again for purchasing this book!

I hope this book was able to help you to understand the basic CSS styling rules.

The next step is to apply what you have just learned in your own webpage.

Finally, if you enjoyed this book, please take the time to share your thoughts and post a review on Amazon. We do our best to reach out to readers and provide the best value we can. Your positive review will help us achieve that. It'd be greatly appreciated!

Thank you and good luck!

Check Out My Other Books

Below you'll find some of my other popular books that are popular on Amazon and Kindle as well. Simply click on the links below to check them out. Alternatively, you can visit my author page on Amazon to see other work done by me.

Android Programming in a Day

Python Programming in a Day

C Programming Success in a Day

C Programming Professional Made Easy

JavaScript Programming Made Easy

PHP Programming Professional Made Easy

C ++ Programming Success in a Day

Windows 8 Tips for Beginners

HTML Professional Programming Made Easy

**Programming Box Set #82: Android Programming in a Day & CSS
Programming Professional Made Easy**

If the links do not work, for whatever reason, you can simply search for these titles on the Amazon website to find them.